Google Adwords Secrets Exposed

GOOGLE ADWORDS SECRETS EXPOSED!

How you can navigate the complicated world of online marketing and come out on top.

BY JEREMY OVERTURF

COPYRIGHT 2016 JEREMY OVERTURF

ALL RIGHTS RESERVED.

NO PART OF THIS BOOK MAY BE USED OR REPRODUCED IN ANY MANNER WHATSOEVER WITHOUT WRITTEN PERMISSION FROM THE AUTHOR.

THANK YOU FOR RESPECTING THE HARD WORK OF THIS AUTHOR.

WWW.JEREMYOVERTURF.COM

Google Adwords Secrets Exposed

How You Can Navigate the
Complicated World of Online
Marketing and
Come Out on Top

Jeremy Overturf

DISCLAIMER

This book is in no way affiliated with or sponsored by Google or its companies.

This book is NOT legal or accounting advice. No earnings claims are being made anywhere in this book or in the marketing of this book. The publisher of this book is not liable for any damages or losses associated with the content of this book.

You are responsible for the advertising and budget of your business. You are responsible for doing your own due diligence and testing.

While we try to keep the information up-to-date and correct, there are no representations or warranties, express or implied, about the completeness, accuracy, reliability, suitability or availability with respect to the information, products, services, or related graphics contained in this book for any purpose. Any use of this information is at your own risk.

Table of Contents

Introduction	1
Secret # 1. Know who your target market is.	6
Secret # 2. Which items should you be advertising on Adwords?	9
Secret # 3. Track it.	12
Secret # 4. Have the right landing page.	14
Secret # 5. Decide what your goal is with the ad.	16
Secret # 6. Study and test headlines.	19
Secret # 7. Keyword strategies	25

**Secret # 8. Tell Adwords when to
run your ads.**   **33**

**Secret #9. Effectively setting up
ad groups.**   **35**

What else should I know?   **38**

Summary   **41**

Introduction

If you've been in business very long, you've no doubt had someone call you and tell you they can get you on the first page of Google. Why does this scam still work? Because the world of online marketing can be confusing and complicated.

On the other hand, you know online marketing can be effective because you buy things online all the time. By picking up this book, you've hopefully done the research and decided that Google Adwords will be an effective advertising tool for your business. So how can you better utilize online marketing? This book will share with you some things that have worked well for me and my companies.

Who am I? I'm an entrepreneur, a small business owner with all kinds of experience when it comes to marketing and making sales. Our company is one of the largest independently owned carpet & floor cleaning companies in our area (west central Florida), we're a Chamber of Commerce Small Business of the Year award winner, and it's quite a successful business operating since 2008. I've used Adwords for other companies I've operated though, and found common threads for getting great results.

Right now, our service company markets with mailers, e-mails, referral programs, but we always get a nice amount of work from Google Adwords. My returns usually average around 8 to 1. I noticed that many others I talked to about this tool have either tried it and were frustrated with it, or were to intimidated and just paid a middle-man to take care of it for them.

This is a guide to getting the most out of your Adwords account. My goal is to help you stop wasting money or getting frustrated with Adwords, because it really can be a great tool once you know how to use it. It will take some practice and knowledge to get it right though. Like any tool, someone can teach you how a hammer works or they can teach you to build beautiful houses. I will not be teaching you how the hammer works in this guide.

This book assumes you have a basic knowledge of how to use Google Adwords: what it is, how to set up an account, add keywords and ads, and create groups. This is not a technical guide. There are several great books for that already, and some wonderful tutorials online with pictures and videos.

I call my tips 'secrets' because most of them have been discovered through trial and error. Many of them are contrary to what you would think, and some even contrast with Google's suggestions. The bottom line is that these ideas work, and I regularly enjoy great returns in my companies. I use these strategies especially in my main service company, but Adwords works in all kinds of industries and companies. If you sell online or just want to get noticed online, Adwords may be a great fit for you. Another nice advantage is that your ads can start showing up at the top of the paid section of Google in just a few hours. The key to this guide is making sure that showing up there doesn't rack up huge bills without a great return on your money.

How did I learn all of this? I've been using Adwords since 2006 with great success. I've also made a lot of mistakes, which helped me develop many of the processes I'm going to explain to you. With a little adjustment it will work for you too.

I am confident you can benefit from some of the ideas in this book to bring greater profits to your business and a more abundant life for your family. I know because I was one of those people that wasted a lot of money on Adwords and gave up on it for several years.

When I first started my service company, I was very price oriented and my main USP (unique selling proposition) was that I was an owner/operator. The page on my website that my ads directed potential customers to explained clearly what I did and had the prices listed. That's what I used in my Adwords ads, and Adwords worked just fine.

Later, I shifted my company to a higher level of service which translated to a higher price. I also shifted to employees instead of owner / operator. Now all of a sudden I was paying hundreds of dollars every month and not getting one Adwords call. Mind you, this was the same ad that was pulling 10 to 1 returns on my investment before my company changed. Why wasn't Adwords working for me anymore? Was it no longer an effective marketing tool?

I decided to do some experimenting. It was too valuable of a marketing tool to just give up on. So I played with different ads, different keywords.

I needed to find some fundamental strategies that could apply no matter what my business was, or no matter how many changes they made to the Adwords platform. That's what led to the creation of this book.

So what is your plan when it comes to Google Adwords? You do have a plan, right? Are you trying to build an e-mail list? Sell online? Get phone calls? Give an introductory offer to work towards a larger sale? As Stephen Covey said, "begin with the end in mind".

Write down your ideal goals for Google Adwords (Secret 5). Figure out what a good return on your money would be, whether monetarily or e-mail list sign-ups. What would have to happen for you to consider it a success? Are you willing to spend the time to track and test it?

You're going to have to do some testing which likely means spending some money you won't see a return on, especially in the beginning.

There is risk involved with any advertising. You can view this as money wasted, but I view it as investing in your education. Sometimes you spend to see what works, just make sure you're not spending money you can't afford to lose. I can't take away that risk, but I can help you manage it better by showing you some of the mistakes I made and how to avoid them.

Once you know your overall goals, it's time to develop your strategy. That's where this book comes in.

For me, ultimately I realized that by upping my prices and changing my service level I was now appealing to a different target market. This market would respond to different messages, so now I needed to discover what those messages were and how to reach them.

Also, you should know Adwords is only one tool in your marketing toolbox. It is not a magic bullet, but can be a nice piece of the puzzle.

What is holding you back from being successful at Adwords?

Let me share with you my top secrets when using Adwords.

Secret # 1

Know who your target market is.

And if you said something like "mine is everybody with a house" or "everyone who likes chocolate" or something else so broad and generic that you are encompassing most of the population, then you don't know your target market. Until you figure this one out, put this book away and come back to it later. Adwords will get very expensive, very quickly for you without you making a dime.

I want you to know it to the level of detail that the major companies do. OK, well you'll probably never know it to that level without their research budgets, but you can get a good idea.

So you might say men and women both purchase your product, rich and poor, and so on. How can you narrow it down? Think about your ideal client, the one you make the most money with. Who spends the most on your product? Who buys it again and again? Who do you enjoy working for? Are they all at a certain location? Are they all in a certain type of industry? What kind of hobbies might they have in common? See how you'll begin to paint a picture?

Now is not the time to be politically correct, each age, gender, race, income bracket, etc. will have messages that appeal specifically to them. If you don't know who you're speaking to, your message will be watered down and weak and won't reach anybody.

Do you think sporting goods stores should know if their major market is men, 18-35 with disposable income? Or are they going after the over 50 market, knowing that they make higher profit margins on the golfers in the area? Would you try to sell an 18 year old a basketball the same as you would a 65 year old a set of golf clubs?

Would you try to appeal to a market that just doesn't have the disposable income to justify your marketing expense? Are you starting to see why finding out this information is helpful?

It may seem counter intuitive, but the more narrow your market the better. After all, as my business coach likes to say, "You get rich in the niche."

In the example of my service company, a homeowner that is willing to pay more means that they value service over price. So an Adwords message that advertises price first will not appeal to that person, it will not even occur to them to click it. Now if you're going after a budget minded consumer where quality is further down the list and price is first, by all means put a special price in your ad. Many fast food places use this strategy.

Something to beware of is making assumptions about who your target market is. Surveys, looking at sales data, and other reports specific to your industry may give you the hard numbers to help you determine this.

The point is, know your audience, know your market, and know what appeals to them. Market research doesn't just consist of what you personally like.

We're not going to do anything with this information yet, but know it so when we get to the next steps you'll be ready.

Secret # 2

Determine which items you should be advertising on Adwords.

If you decide you want to go after more than one of your target markets, narrow them down and segment them into different ad groups. Then you can decide if one is out performing the other, or if one has higher profit margins.

That's what I do, I put more of my budget towards my higher profit margin items, and spend little to nothing on the low margin items. If my ad costs $6 per click but I only make a $10 profit on the item, and it takes 10 clicks to make a sale, should I be advertising this item? Probably not, unless this is an item you're going to make monthly sales on, like a subscription based product. That's where knowing your client acquisition cost is helpful, but that's beyond the scope of this book.

So in our sporting goods example, you would want separate ad groups that would appeal to older golfers then the ads you would have for younger basketball players. Different keywords specific to the sport, and different messages for the age range you're targeting.

Now a few months go by and you track your numbers. You discover that you're spending $500 per month on basketball ads but you're not selling much in that department. You also see that you're only spending $250 per month on golf ads but you're selling $1500 on golf equipment that you've *directly linked to your Google ads*. Now it's time for the next test. If you increase your spending on the golf ads to $500 per month, do you increase your sales to a profitable return on your investment? Track it a few months. If sales have increased enough to justify the extra expense, see if you can raise it again. Keep doing it until your returns are no longer where you need them to be, then back it off to your last profitable configuration. Of course, you will need to keep good records of each change so you will know what to revert back to.

And that basketball ad? Maybe it's time to shut it down if the return isn't there. You'll never know if you don't track it. Just because an item sells well, doesn't mean it will sell well with Adwords.

Of course, before you shut it down, you may need to rewrite your ad, try some different keywords, or try some of the other suggestions we'll get into here. Keep reading.

We have some services in our area where the competition is so great for that service that the cost of some of the keywords has gone up to where it is no longer profitable. I have a maximum CPC (cost per click) set for these keywords where I need to be, and if I don't get any clicks on them I'm not losing any sleep. I know I have other services with barely any competition in my same company. On these services, the keyword bid price stays very low, and the profit margin is great on these services. So I focus more of my attention on these groups in my Adwords account.

Secret # 3

Track it.

So many business owners I've talked to don't track their advertising well. I see their ad somewhere and I ask them how it's doing for them. They usually say, 'great'. My next question is, 'how do you know?' Then the typical response is, 'a lot of people say they saw it.'

If this is how you're running your ad campaigns, stop it. You are throwing money away. As marketing and business legend John Wanamaker famously said, "Half the money I spend on advertising is wasted; the trouble is I don't know which half." Well you may not know exactly, but you can get a good idea with this complicated new system: ASK

Yes, make it part of your script, whether you own a restaurant, an online store, or a bowling alley. Have you been here before? How did you find out about us?

That simple question will save you thousands of dollars and perhaps make you many thousands more.

This is great for making any advertising decision. Recently a magazine we were advertising in asked for our annual renewal. I ran the numbers and found our customer acquisition cost was $100 for every new client from this ad. Now for this industry I knew that was a big number. I also could find the number of clients from that ad that had used our service more than once. So in this case the numbers made the decision for me. And they can do the same for you with Adwords.

Other ways to track:

- Your Adwords landing page has an online form with a code built into it, so if someone submits it, you know it came from that campaign. The same strategy can be used with a specific e-mail address used for Adwords.
- You have a certain phone number on your landing page that tells you it's from your Adwords ad. This is a common way companies track coupons used.

My client management software allows me to enter the source for each new client. Then I can run reports and see what sources all my invoices have come from. Do you think that's a valuable tool? I can see exactly where to put more dollars and where to spend less.

Keep great records, track your numbers, and if you don't have the eye for details to do this find someone who does. Get organized and treat your business like a business, not a hobby.

Secret # 4

Have the right landing page.

What is a landing page? Each ad you create in Adwords can link to a different page on your website. If someone searches Google for a table, they see your ad about a table, click on it and it takes them to your company's furniture homepage, chances are they will click the back arrow and move on.

What if they did a search for a table, saw your ad about a table, then clicked on it and it took them to a page on your furniture website that was specifically about tables? Or maybe even a specific type of table that they searched for? Think about it from your own perspective…isn't this what you were looking for?

In Adwords, you can set up groups narrowed down that specifically. You can have an ad that says, "Looking for a round table?" based on a keyword search of "round table". Yes, it will take you a bit of time to set up, but the return on your investment may be well worth it. Test it.

Some marketers have mastered the art of the landing page. What your potential customer sees that first 30 seconds (or less) can decide if they're spending money with you or not. Have something compelling above the fold, meaning the top of the page before the person has to scroll down. Yes, many people will not even scroll down if you do not capture their attention right away.

Landing pages need to help you reach your goal. If your goal is to sell, your landing page should sell. If you want to gather e-mail addresses, your landing page should be set up to capture them.

The point I'm trying to make here is be intentional as to where you direct people. After all, you're paying for the Adwords ad, make the best use of it. Test different landing pages; see if one gets a better response. There is no one size fits all, but there are basic guidelines and the rest is up to you.

If your landing page sucks, your Adwords ad won't be productive.

Secret # 5

Decide what your goal is with the ad.

"If you aim at nothing, you will hit it every time."
– Zig Ziglar

What is your goal with the ad? That will determine the content of the ad, what you have on your landing page, and your marketing strategy. Some are looking to capture e-mail addresses, others a direct order, others a request for more information or a phone call.

Some have a primary goal, then a secondary goal. For instance, my service company's primary goal is to generate a phone call. Because I know that is my goal, I have set up my Adwords account around that goal. For instance, I've set up a schedule for my Adwords to run only during my business hours. That way I'm not wasting money on ads designed to generate a phone call when no one is in the office.

How else are my ads set up around that goal? The actual text of the Adwords ad is designed to appeal to people ready to have service done (see Secret 1). For instance, I might try an ad with a question like, "Looking for a highly rated carpet cleaner?" This implies they're actively searching to hire a carpet cleaner. I love questions in my ads by the way, more on that later.

However, I also have a secondary goal. If they do not call right away, I have offers and forms to capture their information and get them on my list. Then we they are ready to call, we have been in contact with them and we are the company that is on the top of their minds.

Design your ad and your landing page around a primary and a secondary goal, and make it easy for people to do what you want them to do. If you want them to call, make it easy for them to find a phone number. Put it at the top of the page, the bottom of the page, the sidebar, in the text, and so on. If the secondary goal is to get their information for later, have an email capture form, and make it obvious and easy to find too.

Eye tracking studies reveal things like people viewing web sites starting with the top left, they scan the larger text items, too much bold text causes them to ignore all of it, and so on. Do your homework so you direct people where you want them, and you aren't losing them on the unimportant.

Google "how people view websites" for some fascinating research that can improve your marketing.

If you don't have a clear direction with your ad and with your landing page yet, don't start until you do. If you don't know what you want your visitor to do when they get to your page, how should they know?

Secret # 6

Study and test headlines.

The text ad is what I'm going to go into more detail on here. Primarily because in my own experience it's the one I've had the most success with.

Use the "search network only" when you set up your campaign.

Don't mess with the display ads, image ads, etc. Go with the text ads. Once you've got the search network down, you can test other types of ads like display ads if you want. My text ads are successful enough where I don't need to use the others. I've tried them and they didn't work as well for me.

Think of your text ad as a headline, like you would see in a magazine or an online news article. You know how you can't resist clicking on that headline that says "You won't believe what your favorite 80's star (insert famous name here) looks like now"? A compelling, well written headline is hard to resist, even more so when it's specific to what they've just searched for. Remember how we talked about being specific in secret 4?

I like questions in my ads.

Why? Because it's hard not to answer a question. Go up to a stranger and ask them what time it is. I bet they will give you some type of answer, even if it's a rude one. In fact, I bet you've been answering a lot of the questions I've asked you in this book, at least in your head, haven't you?

When they answer, you have now engaged them in a conversation. It is no longer a one way talking *at* someone, but a two-way talking *with* them. This is a huge difference when it comes to the world of sales and marketing. You know this because you've had a salesperson at some point just not shut up and let you get a word in. Because of their style, you couldn't wait for the 'conversation' to be over.

What type of question should you ask? A simple one with just a few words. Something that stands out from the competition. Follow the example of some of the most memorable ad campaigns of our time. I bet you still know some of the companies that used these:

- Got milk?
- Can you hear me now?
- Do you Yahoo?

- This is your brain. This is your brain on drugs. Any questions?
- What would you do for a Klondike bar?
- Where's the beef?
- How many licks does it take to get to the center of a Tootsie Roll Pop?
- Is it live, or is it Memorex?
- Pardon me. Do you have any Grey Poupon?

Many of these questions instantly invoke an image in your mind. The best ads do. You can picture the actor staring at the hamburger wondering why it's so small.

Ads that are too wordy or complicated won't be remembered. It's a bonus if you can make it catchy and sticky like the hook of a pop song that you can't get out of your head.

Succinctly state your USP (unique selling proposition) in your headline if possible.

If your USP is that your tables are handcrafted, work that into the headline or question. 'Looking for a quality, handcrafted round table?'

No matter what you put, you want a headline that stands out.

Google is a crowded space, and there are lots of competing ads. What makes yours different? Does your headline appeal to your target market from Secret # 1? Can it be unique enough to your company so that your competition couldn't use it because they don't offer what you do? Or are you just marketing __(insert product name here)__ for $__(insert price here)__? That doesn't tell anyone anything except how to compare your price to someone else. Price is not a USP.

What main message do you want your target market to get from your ad in just a few words?

After your initial question or statement, have a call to action.

You will put this in the 'description' section of your text ad. Examples are: Call today! Click here. Book your trip now.

You might want to have a special offer here, if your company does special offers.

Yes, a call to action may seem trivial and overdone, but they really do work. For a great example of a call to action, go to www.JeremyOverturf.com and scroll down to sign up for your free copy of my powerful goal setting program and weekly newsletter.

See how I did that there?

With internet advertising, your goal should be to get someone to take some type of action immediately. You're not trying to build brand awareness with a Google ad, you're trying to generate a phone call, an online order, or get them on your e-mail list. That's why the call to action is so important.

One recent study found a 90 percent better conversion rate using first-person language, e.g., "Start my free trial" vs. "Start your free trial."

To optimize or not to optimize?

There is an option in the settings to rotate your ads evenly or let Google optimize the ones that are performing the best and show them more. Personally, I like to rotate the ads evenly. That way I can see what people are clicking on for myself and not rely on Google's testing and monitoring. Also, just because an ad is generating conversions does not mean it is generating leads. Sometimes ads that have a low click through rate actually perform quite well. Not that many people click on them, but the ones that do are serious buyers. Some of my ads are so specific that they have a low click through rate but they are very successful ads because when people do click on them that money is not wasted on window shoppers.

There are some wonderful books out there on creating headlines and ads. Some of my favorites: "Macy's, Gimbels, and Me" by Bernice Fitz-Gibbon, "Words that Sell" by Richard Bayan, and pretty much anything by Dan Kennedy.

Further testing.

I like to test my ads to the point where I will create two of the exact ad in the same group. Exactly the same except one Has the First Letter of Each Word Capitalized and the other only Has the first letter of the first word capitalized. Sometimes I will test having punctuation on the end of one ad and leave it off on another. Try it for yourself, sometimes I've seen an ad get more clicks with one small change like this than its sister ad that doesn't have it.

Secret # 7

Keyword strategies

So like anything else I tell you in this book, test it for yourself. I'm going to share some tips that I found when it comes to keywords.

Broad match is the devil. You will spend so much money on broad match keywords that you will grow to hate Adwords if you are using them. Google's definition of broad match keywords is : "**Broad match** lets a keyword trigger your ad to show whenever someone searches for that phrase, similar phrases, singular or plural forms, misspellings, synonyms, stemmings (such as floor and flooring), related searches, and other relevant variations." Broad match keywords don't have any punctuation around them.

Basically your ads are going to show up a lot. While that may sound like a good thing, you are going to hit your budget really quick with less than serious buyers and not have anything to show for it.

Your other options are phrase match and exact match. Here are Google's definitions for each:

"Phrase match. A keyword setting that allows your ad to show only when someone's search includes the exact phrase of your keyword, or close variations of the exact phrase of your keyword, with additional words before or after." Phrase match keywords will have quotation marks around them.

"Exact match is a Google AdWords match type which allows you to show your ad only when a searcher types the exact word or phrase you signify in your account. An exact match keyword in Google AdWords ad will only trigger on an exact match search." Exact match keywords have brackets around them.

Phrase match is my weapon of choice. I like the flexibility since my ad will only appear when a user searches for my exact keyword phrase, in its exact order, but maybe with some additional words at the beginning and the end.

So if my keyword is "carpet cleaning" in phrase match, my ads will show for users searching for "best carpet cleaning", "carpet cleaning methods", but not for "clean carpets" or "carpet cleaners". I like phrase match because it's a bit more flexible than exact match, but not as wild west as broad match.

Narrow down your keywords.

In my above example, "carpet cleaning" may be a bit too broad of a keyword, even in phrase match. I might be selling carpet cleaning services in my town but show up in search results for another state. I also could get the phrase match "carpet cleaning" when someone searches for "do it yourself carpet cleaning", which would likely not be my target client. How could I avoid these 2 scenarios?

Location settings.

If you're a local service, be sure you're targeting your specific town. If you're an online service that targets the entire U.S., be sure your ads are not showing up in Japan. You can target narrowed down all the way to zip code, which for my service company is ideal since I can target the zip codes that use our service the most and are most convenient for us to travel to. This is an area that newbies often overlook, one that can cost a lot of money if you're getting clicks in a town or state that you don't serve.

Negative keywords.

These are one of the most important settings of your campaigns, but they are often the most overlooked. Negative keywords are words that if typed into the search cause your ads not to be shown. What a lifesaver these are when using broad or phrase match.

How do these work? Being in the service industry, my company uses the negative keywords "DIY" and "do it yourself" among others. I know if these words are used in any searches, these people are typically searching for instructions on how to do the work for themselves. You might be thinking, "wouldn't these be a good potential customer if they aren't able to figure it out themselves?" Maybe in some industries, but not mine. I would rather spend that money on someone looking to hire a service company. We're after the low hanging fruit here, not spending all day trying to convert atheists.

You can set up negative keywords at either the ad group level or the campaign level. You would set it up at the ad group level if you wanted the words to show up on some ads in your campaign and not show up on others.

At this point you may be thinking, why are you spending so much time and effort getting people not to see your ads? Getting people to see your ads on Google Adwords is not difficult. The art is in getting the right people to see your ads. Negative keywords ensure your money is being spent in the best possible way.

To be safe, add negative keywords as exact match (with "quotes"). This gives you the most control and limits how broadly your negative prevents ads from displaying. Of course, some words, like 'jobs' and 'download,' may be safe to add as broad negatives.

How do you know if you need to add more negative keywords?

Let's say you're getting a lot of clicks but none of the action steps you're hoping for with your ads. Take a look at Google Analytics, a great free reporting tool for your website. This will tell you how people found your website and what search terms they used. So if they found you through a phrase match and you see their search is not related to what you offer, now you have a clue that this may need to be a negative keyword in your campaign.

Let's use an example so it makes more sense. You had 5 clicks today but no orders. Google Analytics shows that your phrase "round table" was showing up when someone searched "knights of the round table". This search doesn't help you sell tables and you can't imagine that it ever will. So now you might consider adding "knights" as a negative keyword so this won't happen again.

If you're not comfortable with Google Analytics, AdWords can generate a report with all search terms that were used by multiple people and received clicks in the past 30 days.

The Search Terms Report

I know I said this wasn't a technical manual, but I am including instructions on how to find this report, since it's well hidden.

To generate your AdWords search terms report:

1. Click the **Campaigns** tab.
2. Click the **Keywords** tab.
3. Click the **Search Terms** button.
4. Click the download button to export the data.

These exact instructions are subject to change, as Google often likes to switch things up.

The Search Terms Report will save you money. This report provides you with a complete report on the search terms that caused your ads to display. It also shows how they performed. The key is you're seeing search terms as opposed to keywords. Based on this data, you can determine which terms should be added to your keywords for a particular ad or ad group.

So as regards negative keywords, a particular search term may be driving a lot of traffic, but is too general or resulting in a high bounce rate. Add it to your negative keyword list. That way, you won't waste valuable impressions or pay for clicks on terms for which your ad is irrelevant like our table example above.

This report has some other interesting data about your activity, such as your competitor's rankings.

Find new keyword opportunities

Google has a free tool, Keyword Planner. Using it, you can research:

- Keyword ideas based on a phrase, landing page or product category
- Average monthly search volume for a specific period
- Search volume trends for a single keyword or group of keywords over time

You will be presented with a few options when you use this tool.

Search for new keywords using a phrase, website or category

This tool generates lists of keywords from an initial keyword (or list of keywords), a landing page URL or a product category.

The list it generates will include search volume and trend data.

Get search volume data and trends in Keyword Planner

This tool lets you upload an existing list of keywords to get volume and trend data.

Multiply keyword lists to get new keywords

The keyword multiplier tool can create large lists of keywords. It does so when you enter lists of phrases and it then generates all possible combinations of terms.

Get click and cost performance forecasts

With the forecast tool, you can upload a list of keywords and get forecasted clicks and impressions based on a specific budget and targeting criteria.

Don't add everything

Use this tool to get ideas to build your keyword list, but remember to keep your target market and goal in mind as you add new keywords. Your goal isn't to show up for every search, but to show up for the right searches.

There are numerous online tutorials for using this tool. Keyword Planner will be available once you have an active Adwords account. Play around with it; use it from time to time if you are not getting enough activity on your account or when you add a new product or service. Remember to add the new words as phrase match, not the default broad match. Phrase match will have quotation marks around the keyword.

Secret # 8

Tell Adwords when to run your ads.

You may not want to run your ads 24 hours a day. As my above example, I've found my money is best spent by running them during my office hours so someone can answer the phone calls.

Once you've determined when your ads are most successful, you can set up a schedule accordingly. Another reason to pay attention to time, you can adjust your bids depending on the time of day. Increase your bids during competitive times and lower your bids when traffic slows to maximize your budget while maintaining a top position.

Would a weight loss product do better at night? A productivity tool during work hours? This comes back to knowing your products and your audience.

Here are the steps for Adwords Ads Scheduling

1. Under All campaigns, click the name of the campaign you want you edit.
2. Select the Settings tab.
3. Review your campaign "Type." ...
4. Under "Additional settings," click Schedule: Start date, end date, ad scheduling.
5. Next to your current start date, click Edit. ...
6. Enter your start date, then click Save.

You can even determine what days of the week you are having a higher traffic and a higher conversion rate. For that, all you need to do is go over to the Dimensions Tab and hover on top of Time and then click on Day of the Week.

If your ads have a high conversion rate on Wednesdays for example, then you may want to increase your budget for those days.

Secret #9

Effectively setting up ad groups.

There are different strategies that work well when setting up your ad groups. Google recommends 10-20 keywords per ad group, and in some cases that works just fine.

In my carpet cleaning company, I have my groups broken out by services that the company provides: a group with general carpet cleaning keywords, one for tile cleaning, Oriental rug cleaning, and so on. However, I did test a more specific group that has done very well, 'carpet cleaning reviews'. Now when people do searches related to reviews of carpet cleaners, that group takes them to our page of customer reviews.

The more specific you can get the better. In fact too many keywords per ad group can make search-to-ad message match hard to achieve. Here's why.

Message match is when the search term matches with the ad, and it's ideal because achieving it means that Google bolds your matching ad copy and it really stands out.

But when you have too many keywords in an ad group, you won't ever have a 100% message match between the keyword being searched and the ad that is being triggered to show. The ad will be too general, not specific enough to the keyword. For instance, if we wanted to do our 'round table' ad, someone searched 'round table' but we had that keyword with every other 'table' keyword in our ad group, then we would just have a general 'table' related ad, and it wouldn't stand out. It wouldn't say that your page or your ad was about round tables specifically. So what do you do?

One strategy is called Single keyword ad groups (aka SKAGs). SKAGs allow you to control the message match between the keyword and the text ad because only one keyword will trigger that specific ad.

When you only have one keyword per ad group, you can make your ad extremely specific to that keyword. So someone that searched for 'round table' might see your ad that says:

Looking for a round table?
You'll love our selection of the finest round tables in St. Louis.
Order online or visit our downtown location.

Do you see how much more specific that is? Do you think that might catch someone's eye when it looks like the search results are catered exactly for what they were looking for?

As you set up these ad groups, don't forget about your negative keywords. When you start extremely specific in your groups, negative keywords become even more important and you may need to set them up at the group level instead of campaign level or account level. This will then prevent your short tail keywords stealing away impressions from the longer tail ones if you're doing single keyword ad groups. Yes, we're getting very specific here and you may need some further research and testing if you want to implement the SKAGs strategy.

You may not need to get that specific to have excellent results, but this may be the perfect strategy for your business. I have my negative keywords set up at the campaign level, and I've grouped my keywords a little more generally as I outlined at the beginning of this chapter. Still I've made them specific enough to have relevant ads to the search the user is performing.

What else should I know about Adwords?

Any other secrets?

A few other things:

You're going to have to test your **budget and max cost per click**.

A $5 bid per keyword in your hometown may be plenty, or it may not get you on the first page. Showing up past the 3rd position is pretty much useless. It will take some time to see how your keywords do with the budget you set, so watch for keywords that aren't showing up because your budget is too low and decide if it's worth it to you to spend more.

Decide how much you are comfortable spending each day, then wait and see if that's enough. Just because you would like to spend $5 per day doesn't mean that it's a good idea. You won't get enough data to make any real decisions if you don't spend enough on your testing.

Consider long tail keywords.

Long-tail keywords are longer and more specific keyword phrases that visitors are more likely to use when they're closer to a point-of-purchase. They might seem strange, but they can be very valuable if you know how to use them.

For example: if you're a company that sells Pez dispensers, the chances are that your pages are never going to appear near the top of an organic search for "candy" because there's too much competition (this is particularly true if you're a smaller company or a startup). But if you specialize in, say, Star Wars Pez dispensers, then keywords like "Darth Vader Pez" are going to reliably find customers looking for exactly that product (and be much cheaper since the competition will be lower).

There are advanced options like Ad Extensions and Dynamic Keyword Insertion that you may find very useful.

They will take some more time to set up but may be worth the research. The level of depth Adwords contains is impressive, but you could also waste a lot of time trying to get it perfect and explore every feature. Sometimes it's better to get started then to wait until all the lights are green to head into town.

Should you run mobile ads?

Yes. Click the option for your ads to be shown on mobile devices. Pretty soon that's where most of the searches will be taking place so you will be missing most of your audience if you do not. Make sure your site is mobile optimized as well so it looks good on a cell phone.

If you're getting 8 to 1 returns why don't you just spend $1 million and make $8 million?

Believe me, the thought has crossed my mind, and maybe it will work for you. In the testing I've done, I've discovered that there is usually a point where the return begins to diminish no matter how much higher the budget is set. By all means, if Adwords is working for you, keep testing it at higher budgets and see if the returns are still there.

Summary

A common theme you probably noticed in almost all of these strategies is testing. Something that works wonders in your industry, in your hometown, or with your target market may fail miserable in my company. That doesn't mean Adwords won't work for me and it doesn't mean this book won't work. You can't just clone someone else's campaigns, and really that's the beauty of why it works.

When we talk about general fundamentals like we've outlined here though, the strategies apply in the majority of cases.

If your ads aren't performing, it may be just a little adjustment that you need to make. Get some feedback from someone you trust and see if you're following the suggestions here. **If you see something is not performing over time, get rid of it.** Whether an ad, a keyword, or even an entire group.

As with any marketing, run reports and check your ROI (return on investment) from time to time, making sure nothing has changed drastically. Fine tune it, but if it's not broke, don't fix it. Google may call you and suggest changes, but no matter what their intentions, if you're getting good returns don't mess with it too much. I know this from experience, the Google reps advice may not get you the results you're hoping for.

I'm confident that when you put these tips together and apply them to your specific situation, you'll create an automatic marketing machine. Invest the time and energy today and your investment will pay off for years to come.

I wish you the best with your marketing, whether your business is small or large, and I hope this book can serve as a helpful tool in your toolbox.

About the author:

Jeremy Overturf is a speaker, author, and entrepreneur. He lives in Southwest Florida outside of Sarasota with his wife Stefanie. Together they run an award winning carpet and floor cleaning company along with many other successful business ventures.

Find out more and get more resources for entrepreneurs at:

www.JeremyOverturf.com

www.facebook.com/jeremyoverturf

www.ingramcontent.com/pod-product-compliance
Lightning Source LLC
Chambersburg PA
CBHW070411190526
45169CB00003B/1204